You Can Draw

Cats!

Katie Dicker

Gareth Stevens
Publishing

Please visit our website, www.garethstevens.com. For a free color catalog of all our high-quality books, call toll free 1-800-542-2595 or fax 1-877-542-2596.

Library of Congress Cataloging-in-Publication Data

[publication data illegible]

ISBN 978-1-4339-8727-4 (library binding)
ISBN 978-1-4339-8728-1 (6-pack)
ISBN 978-1-4339-8726-7 (library binding)
1. Cartooning—Juvenile literature. 2. Drawing—Technique—Juvenile literature. I. Title.
NC1320.
741.2—dc23

2012035152

Published in 2013 by
Gareth Stevens Publishing
111 East 14th Street, Suite 349
New York, NY 10003

Contents

You Can Draw Cats!

There are many different cat breeds. Some cats, such as ragdolls and Maine coons, have long, thick coats of fur. Other cats, such as Abyssinians and Siamese cats, are covered in short, fine hair. Every type of cat has special needs. Some like to be outdoors, while other cats love being inside. Find out how to care for many different cat breeds—and how to draw them, too.

Discover how to draw cats!

🐾 Follow the steps that show you how to draw each type of cat. Then draw from a photograph of your own pet to create a special pet portrait!

🐾 You Will Need:
- Art paper and pencils
- Eraser
- Coloring pens and/or paints and a paintbrush

🐾 Abyssinians

🐾 Maine coons

🐾 Persians

🐾 Ragdolls

🐾 Siamese cats

🐾 Burmese cats

Persian Cats

Persian cats are cute, gentle cats that love to be around their owner. If you want a cat that loves to be pampered, the Persian could be your perfect choice. These cats are not as curious as some cats such as Abyssinians. Persians prefer to spend their day sleeping and lying around.

Persians are known for their soft, fluffy coat of fur.

Step 1

First, draw the cat's outline. Notice how the Persian is lying, with its forelegs curled under its chest. Pencil the outline of the fur on the cat's back.

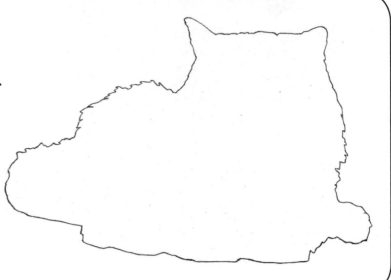

Step 2

Now begin to add detail to your picture. Use light pencil strokes to draw your cat's fluffy coat. Draw fur on the head, ears, back, and the paws of the cat.

Step 3

Draw the eyes, nose, and mouth. Add some fur to the cat's face.

Caring for your Persian

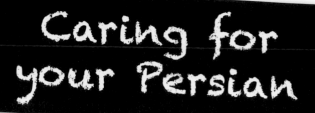

🐾 You will need to brush your cat's coat regularly. Persians have beautiful, long fur that should be combed daily to keep it healthy. Use a fine-wired brush to groom your pet.

🐾 Your Persian may need a bath if its fur becomes very tangled or dirty. Try to bathe your cat regularly so it becomes used to bathtime.

🐾 Because of their long hair, Persians often get hairballs from grooming themselves. You will need to treat your cat with a hairball food formula.

Persians come in lots of colors, including gray, orange, blue, chocolate brown, cream, lilac, and black.

Step 4

Use lots of short pencil strokes to add fur to the rest of the cat. Carefully shade the pupils of the eyes and add detail to the nose.

Step 5

Now use your colored pencils. Use a light gray for the cat's fur. Then use a darker color to add depth and shade. You can add highlights by using your eraser to remove pencil marks. Color the cat's eyes a rich orange and add highlights. Color the nose pink.

Siamese Cats

Constantly talking, Siamese cats love to talk with their owners. These cats talk more than almost any other breed of cat. Siamese cats like to be with their owners and will often follow them around the house.

Siamese cats come in four colors—chocolate brown, lilac, gray, and blue.

Step 1

Carefully draw the shape of your cat. Keep a steady hand as you draw the pointed ear and the paw.

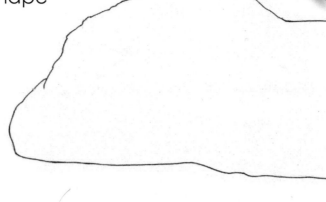

Step 2

Begin to add detail. Draw the shape of the ears and tail, then add the shape of the face and the forelegs. Draw some fur on the back and tail.

Step 3

Draw the cat's eyes, nose, mouth, and the shape of its jaw. Pencil fur around its eyes and on the top of its head. Draw the shape of the claws.

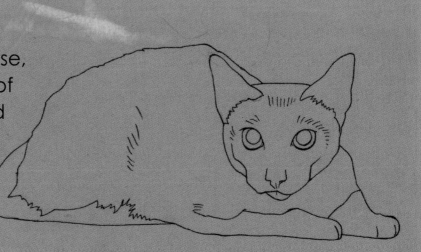

Caring for your Siamese

🐾 If you can, keep two Siamese cats as pets. Another cat will be a friend for your pet and will help it feel safe when you are away.

🐾 Don't leave your Siamese alone for a long time. These friendly cats love company and will be lonely without it.

🐾 Siamese cats are active, smart cats. Give your pet lots of toys such as a scratching post, plastic toys, and balls to keep it happy.

🐾 Show your Siamese plenty of love and affection. These cats love to be loved!

Siamese cats have long, slender bodies and tails.

Step 4

Add short, light strokes for the cat's furry coat. Use a thick-tipped pencil to shade its eyes. Leave two dots unshaded—these will be highlights.

Step 5

Now add color. Use a light brown pencil for some of the fur. Use a dark brown to add shade and to color the ears, tail, face, and legs. Leave areas on the back, hind leg, chest, and head white, as shown below. Use a light blue for the rim of the eyes.

13

Maine Coon Cats

These large cats can grow up to 40 inches (101 cm) long.

Step 1

Carefully, draw the outline of your cat. Notice how it is lying on its side, with its forelegs in front and its rear legs stretched behind.

Step 2

Add the shape of the jaw, ears, and the cat's paws. When you draw the paws, be careful to turn the paw on the right foreleg and the left hind leg inward.

Step 3

Pencil the markings on the face. Add the cat's eyes, nose, and mouth. Draw some fur on the chest and the forelegs.

Caring for your Maine Coon

🐾 Only choose this pet if you have a large backyard, or live in a rural area. Maine coons love to prowl!

🐾 Give your cat a hairball food formula. Like most long-haired cats, Maine coons often get hairballs from grooming themselves.

🐾 Think about keeping another pet as a friend for your cat. Maine coons are friendly animals and get along well with other pets, including dogs.

Maine coons have litters of around four to six kittens.

Step 4

Use short pencil strokes to add lots of lines of fur to the cat's body, head, back, and legs. Carefully shade the pupils of the cat's eyes.

Step 5

Add color with a palette of browns, grays, and black. First color the body with light brown. Then add dark brown to the cat's face, head, and paws. Use black to create the markings on the cat's face, head, and to color its paws. Use a light green for the cat's pretty eyes. Add shade to your picture with a mixture of light and dark gray pencil. You can add highlights by erasing areas of pencil. Finally, use a pale pink color for the cat's nose.

Abyssinian Cats

If you want a playful, fun-loving cat, then the Abyssinian is the pet for you! These cats love to jump, run, and play with toys. Just don't expect to have lots of cuddles with your pet. Abyssinians are high-spirited creatures that like to be on the move all day.

Many Abyssinians have a rich, rusty-brown coat of fur.

Step 1

Draw your cat from the side, with its tail curled behind it. Carefully draw the tall, upright ears, and the arch in the cat's back. Pencil the outline of the cat's dainty paws.

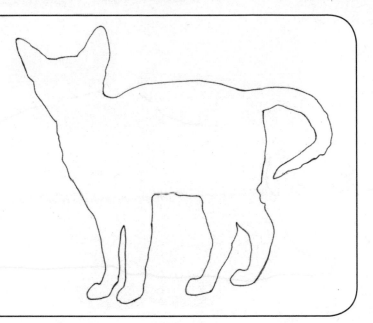

Step 2

Add the shape of the cat's jaws and the ears. Draw the outline of its chest and add detail to the shape of its legs. Carefully, draw the fine lines on the Abyssinian's paws.

Step 3

Now draw the eyes, nose, and mouth. Add small dots around the mouth and nose area. Draw some short lines on the neck and back for fur.

Caring for your Abyssinian

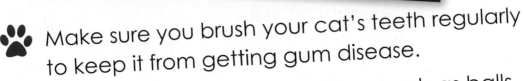

🐾 Make sure you brush your cat's teeth regularly to keep it from getting gum disease.

🐾 Give your playful cat lots of toys such as balls on a piece of string and squeaky plastic mice.

🐾 Abyssinians love their food! Feed your cat regularly.

🐾 These active cats need owners who have backyards.

Give your cute cat lots of fun toys to play with.

Step 4

Shade the pupils and add more short strokes for the fur on the chest, belly, back, head, legs, and the tail. This will create areas of shade and pattern on the Abyssinian's body.

Step 5

Use a palette of rich browns, orange, and black to color your cat. Add shade with a mix of light and dark brown pencil. Give your cat beautiful green eyes. Add white highlights to the ears and the jaw.

Ragdoll Cats

Ragdolls were first bred in California in the '60s. They were named "ragdoll" because they go all "limp as a ragdoll" when picked up or carried. These cats are cute-looking animals, with large, bright blue eyes and beautiful long, thick fur.

Ragdolls come in lots of different colors, from gray, blue, and chocolate to red, cream, and lilac.

Step 1

This ragdoll is sitting in an upright position. Carefully draw the outline of the cat. Keep a steady hand to draw the outline of the pet's ears, and pencil the shape of its paws. Then add some short strokes to create a fluffy tail.

Step 2

Now you can begin to add detail by drawing the lines on the cat's paws. Don't forget to add detail to the ragdoll's ears and forelegs, too.

Step 3

Draw the large, round eyes and the nose and mouth. Add dots to the area around the nose. Pencil some fur on the cat's head.

Caring for your Ragdoll

🐾 Brush your ragdoll's fluffy coat with a fine-wire brush. Remember to groom the coat twice a week to keep it in good condition.

🐾 Ragdolls love to scratch so make sure you give your cat a scratching post. Otherwise, it may scratch your furniture!

🐾 Give your cat a lot of love and affection. Ragdolls love to be petted.

🐾 Ragdolls make great housecats. They are better suited to indoor life than other, hardier cats.

Ragdoll kittens have lots of very soft fur and bushy tails.

Step 4

Carefully shade the eyes and the nose. Leave a circle within each eye white to create a highlight. Add more short pencil strokes on the head, neck, chest, and legs for fur.

Step 5

Color the ragdoll with a soft, light gray. Use a mixture of dark gray and brown for the face, ears, tail, and the paws. Take care to shade the face with a deep gray color, and add the three black markings between the cat's eyes. Also shade the ears, nose, paws, and tail with a deep, dark gray. Add light brown to the forelegs. Give your cute cat beautiful, big blue eyes.

Burmese Cats

Burmese cats love to be around people and to have fun! These playful, loving cats are one of the most popular of cat breeds. Burmese cats are social cats with muscular bodies. They are one of the most playful of breeds. A Burmese likes nothing more than to cuddle with you.

As adults, Burmese cats are agile. As kittens, they can be a little clumsy!

Step 1

This playful cat is sitting upright, with its paw held out as if to say, "Come play with me!" Notice the long lines of the body and legs as you draw the shape of your cat.

Step 2

Now you can add your Burmese's outstretched foreleg. Draw the fur on the foreleg, then add the fine lines on the cat's paws.

Step 3

Draw the round eyes, nose, and mouth. Add dots around the nose and the mouth. Draw a fine line of hair beneath the cat's jaw.

Caring for your Burmese

🐾 Make sure your Burmese has a collar with a name and address tag. Burmese cats need their owner to care for them. They cannot survive easily if they become lost.

🐾 Burmese cats love company. It is a good idea to keep another Burmese as a friend for your cat if your house is empty during the day.

🐾 If you have a male Burmese, it will probably be very laid back. Females Burmese cats tend to be more high-strung and nervous.

Burmese cats are colored brown, blue, creamy beige, or white.

Step 4

Use lots of short, light pencil strokes to add fur all over the cat. Concentrate on the neck area and around the jaw, where the shading will be heaviest. Shade the pupils.

Step 5

Finally, color the cat with a palette of grays. Color most of the cat with a light gray. Then use a darker gray or black to go over the lighter gray to add shading. You can easily add white highlights by erasing areas of pencil. Use this tip to add highlights to the top of the head, legs, paws, nose, and ears. Add some more highlights to the cat's body and tail. To complete your beautiful cat, add emerald-green eyes.

Glossary

active: full of ...

agile: able to easily move

breed: a type of animal, such as a breed of cat

coat: the fur covering on an animal

curious: wanting to find out about things

detail: the features and small features of a picture

food formula: a food mixture that contains certain vitamins, minerals, and other nutrients needed for good health

grooming: cleaning or brushing

gum disease: when the gums are no longer healthy

hairball: a ball of hair that has been swallowed by an animal

hardy: tough

high spirited: lively, fun-loving

high strung: nervous, anxious

house cat: cat that is kept indoors

litter: baby animals born at the same time from one mother

markings: the patterns or colors on a cat's fur when ...

For More Information

Books

Fisher, Diana. *Learn to Draw Cats and Kittens*. Laguna Hills, CA: Walter Foster Publishing, 2012.

Soloff Levy, Barbara. *Aj48A Animals: How to Draw with Simple Shapes*. Mineola, NY: Dover Publications, 2010.

Zobel, Derek. *Caring for Your Cat*. Minneapolis, MN: Bellwether Media, 2010.

Websites

Find out cool facts about each cat.
www.animalleague.org/kids/cool_pet_facts.html

Discover more about how to look after your cat at
www.cfainc.org/client/catlinqu.px

Find out more about cat breeds at
www.cfainc.org

Choose a name for your pet cat at
www.bowwow.com.au

Index